Bilingual Edition

Edición bilingüe

Let's Draw a Truck with Shapes

Vamos a dibujar un camión usando figuras

Joanne Randolph
Illustrations by Emily Muschinske

The Rosen Publishing Group's
PowerStart Press™ & **Editorial Buenas Letras**™
New York

1

Published in 2005 by The Rosen Publishing Group, Inc.
29 East 21st Street, New York, NY 10010

First Edition

Book Design: Emily Muschinske
Photo Credits: pp. 23, 24 © Royalty-Free/Corbis.

Library of Congress Cataloging-in-Publication Data
Randolph, Joanne.
Let's draw a truck with shapes = Vamos a dibujar un camión usando figuras / Joanne Randolph ; translated by Mauricio Velázquez de León ; illustrations by Emily Muschinske.
    p. cm. — (Let's draw with shapes = Vamos a dibujar con figuras)
English and Spanish.
Includes index.
ISBN 1-4042-7554-1 (library binding)
1. Trucks in art—Juvenile literature. 2. Geometry in art—Juvenile literature. 3. Drawing—Juvenile literature. I. Title: Vamos a dibujar un camión usando figuras. II. Muschinske, Emily. III. Title. IV. Let's draw with shapes.
NC825.T76R36 2005b
743'.89629224-dc22
                                                    2004004786

Manufactured in the United States of America

Due to the changing nature of Internet links, PowerStart Press has developed an online list of Web sites related to the subject of this book. This site is updated regularly. Please use this link to access the list:
http://www.buenasletraslinks.com/ldwsh/camion

Contents

Contenido

Draw a red rectangle to start your truck.

Dibuja un rectángulo de color rojo para comenzar tu camión.

Add an orange half circle
and an orange square for the
front of your truck.

Dibuja un semicírculo
y un cuadrado de color
anaranjado para hacer
la parte delantera de
tu camión.

Draw a yellow square for the window of your truck.

Dibuja un cuadrado amarillo para hacer la ventana de tu camión.

Add a green square and a small green rectangle to the front of your truck.

Dibuja un cuadrado y un pequeño rectángulo de color verde para hacer el frente de tu camión.

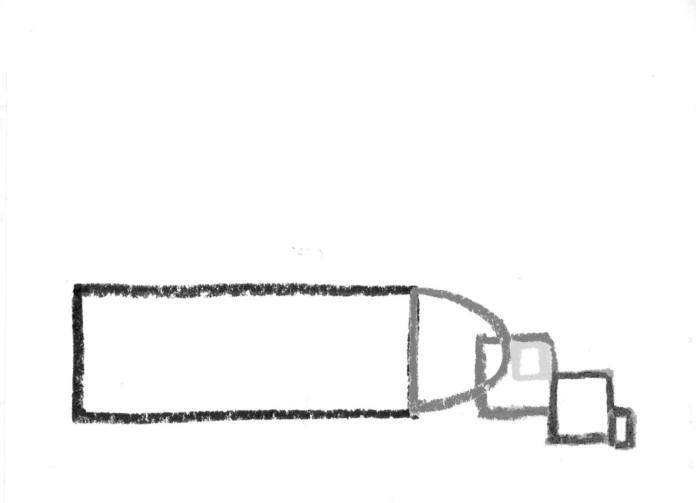

Draw a blue circle to make a wheel on your truck. Add a thin blue rectangle to your truck.

Dibuja un círculo azul para hacer una de las ruedas de tu camión. Agrega un rectángulo azul.

12

Add two purple circles
for some of the wheels on
your truck.

Dibuja dos círculos de
color violeta para hacer
dos ruedas de tu camión.

14

Draw a pink square for the door of your truck.

Dibuja un cuadrado rosa para hacer la puerta de tu camión.

Add two black circles for more wheels.

Dibuja dos círculos negros para hacer el resto de las ruedas.

Color in your truck.

_____

Colorea tu camión.

This truck is an
18-wheeler.

Este camión tiene
18 ruedas.

Words to Know/Palabras que debes saber

18-wheeler/
camión de 18 ruedas

front/frente

wheel/rueda

window/ventana

Colors/ Colors

red/rojo

orange/anaranjado

yellow/amarillo

green/verde

blue/azul

purple/violeta

pink/rosa

black/negro

Shapes/ Figuras

circle/círculo

square/cuadrado

triangle/triángulo

rectangle/rectángulo

oval/óvalo

half circle/semicírculo

Index

Índice